Believe In the Cross

RICHARD PARNES

Other Books by Richard Parnes

Fiction
The Death Maze
The Death Maze 2, The Other Side

Poetry
Peace In Kind

Believe in the Cross
Copyright © 2024 by Richard Parnes

ISBN: 978-1639458646(sc)
ISBN: 978-1639458653 (e)

All rights reserved. No part of this publication may be reproduced, distributed, or transmitted in any form or by any means, including photocopying, recording, or other electronic or mechanical methods, without the prior written permission of the publisher and/or the author, except in the case of brief quotations embodied in critical reviews and other noncommercial uses permitted by copyright law.

The views expressed in this book are solely those of the author and do not necessarily reflect the views of the publisher, and the publisher hereby disclaims any responsibility for them.

Writers' Branding
(877) 608-6550
www.writersbranding.com
media@writersbranding.com

Author's Note

Believe in the Cross is a continuation of my previous book Peace In Kind. There were so many more songs that I did not know at the time if they would be compatible to incorporate into the first book. When I began reading again those "left out pieces of music and lyrics," I realized that I was remiss in my thoughts. Words to me from God and Jesus always fit in with all the work because this is what I'm being told when I write. I knew I had to listen to God and Jesus when they were speaking to me. If not them, then my angels who contact me in church or in Adoration Chapel or in my car while driving…I hope you can understand what I mean.

I also knew that there were many new pieces of music, lyrics and prose coming into my mind. I continue to listen to those special voices within no matter what the time of day or evening it is. Believe in the Cross follows the same pattern with the lyrics written into prose sans music. However, some of the titles were originally written without music.

My goal is to always follow the path that God Almighty and Jesus Christ want of me. I believe I understand that path and do hope that the reader enjoys what I have put down on paper.

May God, Jesus Christ and the Holy Spirit be a part of your lives during the journey of reading Believe in the Cross.

Richard Parnes

P.S. The picture on the cover of the book is my Baptism candle. It is next to my bed when my wife and I pray the rosary every evening. It reminds me of the promise I made to God Almighty, Jesus Christ and the Holy Ghost. It's not only in my heart, but deep within my soul. Blessings!

Table of Contents

Believe In the Cross 1
I Am the Way 5
Into My Heart 9
Just For You 13
Loving You With All My Heart 17
The Triune God 21
This Soul is Yours 25
Universal Consciousness of One 29
It Is Right 33
If We All 37
Teach Me O Lord 41
Eternally 45
Take Away 49
In My Life 53
I Pray to the Lord 55
My Abundance in Life 57
The Lord is Close to Me 59
God's Pure Love 63
Déjà vu 67
Walk a Mile to the Gates of Heaven 69
Maybe 73
Past Strife 75
We Could Be Next 77

You're the Rock I Need 79
Come Alive 81
Because 85
The Maker of the World 89
Let Me Follow 93
A Community of Love 97
Let Me Be... Your Song 101
Glory to God in the Highest 105
Son Our Lord 109
A Thank You Prayer 113

Believe In the Cross

Richard Parnes

I rise up each morning bow my head and say
I thank the Lord for another day…
In my life
He's the King of my soul
Let my heart rejoice, for the words I hear
To be one with God is the message so clear…
To behold

Start singing with Him
And dance with the wind
The gifts He gives us each day
Brings us joy as we pray
There's no shortage of time to embrace and be tossed
Though the rivers and seas join the people…Believe
In the Cross

Repent of past sins stay awake through the night
For the Groom will appear and you may lose sight…
Of the chance
To be one with His Son
For His glory fulfilled, He will soon come again
To all those who believe that the glorious plan
Will be done

Believe In the Cross

Start singing with Him
And dance with the wind
The gifts He gives us each day
Brings us joy as we pray
There's no shortage of time to embrace and be tossed
Though the rivers and seas join the people…Believe
In the Cross

I close my eyes and I hope and I say…
Give thanks to Him in a glorious way
I Believe in the Cross

I Am the Way

Richard Parnes

I am the way
I am the truth
I am the light of the world
I am the proof
Reach deep in your mind
And listen to all that is said
There's nothing that won't come to pass
The words we are fed

Stretch out your hands
Touch the beauty from Him
You will exhibit the radiant life
He will wipe out your sins
Believe in the Son
The gifts that will soon expand
For the way to eternal peace
The love He commands

So shout out for joy
There's no way He will push you aside
The path to redemption in life
For He is your guide
Come forth and bring
All the tears you have shed
For Christ is the way, the truth and life
He is our bread

Believe In the Cross

Let us speak of His life
Let us count all the ways
We should know that the hate of the world
Will deter any praise
For He gave us the tools
To accept all the pain
For the knowledge of hope and life and love
Will wipe all the blame

I am the way
I am the truth
I am the light of the world
I am the proof
I am the way
I am the truth
I am the light of the world
I am God's proof

Into My Heart

Richard Parnes

Oh Lord, oh me
That's not the way I want it to be
I wanted the sun, the moon and the stars
Oh Lord, see why
I keep on trying and yet I fly
Into the deep I seem behind bars

And you, you give me hope
To keep building on and reach for my dream
You never cease
You always strive and break through the screen
But I, I keep acting on
My goal is for us to build all our hopes
I'll never quit, I'll never sit, I'll try not to mope

Oh Lord, oh me
The rainbow shines beyond the sea
We drift on the wave for our pot of gold
Oh Lord, see why
We live forever in our minds
The spirit it shines although we are old

Believe In the Cross

For You, You are my life
You are His Son, you are an angel caring for me
Watching my work, an eternity
And I, I'll never forget that touch or caress
You only dress my life up with lights
A shimmer, a star, You are the best

Oh Lord, oh me
You are my eternal key
You open the door
Into My Heart

Just For You

Richard Parnes

Lord you fill up my heart
Bless my soul with your love
Higher and higher you fill my desire to know more about you
Lord you'll take full control
Teach to walk in your words
Laws and degrees I will follow to please
Just For You

You are my rock
My foundation in life
Whatever the cause, the effect in return is the law, it is right
So do unto those as you'd have done unto you
To labor with love and the ways from above will be true

Lord you fill up my heart
Bless my soul with your love
Higher and higher you fill my desire to know more about you
Lord you'll take full control
Teach to walk in your words
Laws and degrees I will follow to please
Just For You

Believe In the Cross

My life on this Earth
There's a reason you know
What I've done before, a certain folklore, did I learn? Where's the glow?
So try as I may to do only right is my goal
My future will tell, is the picture now well, am I whole?

Lord you fill up my heart
Bless my soul with your love
Higher and higher you fill my desire to know more about you
Lord you'll take full control
Teach to walk in your words
Laws and degrees I will follow to please
Just For You

Loving You With All My Heart

Richard Parnes

Pray for me
I thank the Lord and bless His name for all my needs
Stay with me
The life we lead, the path to take, the gifts to please
Take of my soul
And show me songs of glory to sing your tune
You make me whole
His beauty shines, it builds beyond the evening moon
So I can't disguise the passion in my heart for you
I can only fill the void by praising God for truth
It's a building block we take each day and when we start
And complete the moments Loving You with All My Heart.

Reach out to those
Who in turn could use a helpful hand, the gifts of Him
Words filled with prose
And a smile changes attitudes from deep within
Be part of the cause
That embraces all and shows us of His glorious Son
Spread forth the laws
To eliminate disdain will show we now have won
So I can't disguise the passion in my heart for you
I can only fill the void by praising God for truth
It's a building block we take each day and when we start
And complete the moments Loving You with All My Heart.

Believe In the Cross

Time heals the wounds
We become a people knowing love will win throughout
Free will to choose
That our time in our lives be blessed without the doubt
And know that all
Can depend on Him and see the splendor when we're done
We'll never fall
We'll erase the hate and learn to quote from God's own Son
So I can't disguise the passion in my heart for you
I can only fill the void by praising God for truth
It's a building block we take each day and when we start
And complete the moments Loving You with All My Heart.

Sings songs of joy
Give praise and blessings to His one and only Son.
Cry out and throw away your ploys
That would have you sin and bring repentance when you're done.
Lift up His name
He is first and foremost in all things we do and say.
He bears our shame
We should pray and give thanks to Him for each new day.
So I can't disguise the passion in my heart for you
I can only fill the void by praising God for truth
It's a building block we take each day and when we start
And complete the moments Loving You with All My Heart.

So I can't disguise the passion in my heart for you
I can only fill the void by praising God for truth
It's a building block we take each day and when we start
And complete the moments Loving You with All My Heart.

Pray for me.

The Triune God

Richard Parnes

It is the Father who has made the day and night
Who has formed the world with all the wonders living in our sight
It is the Father who has blessed the world we walk
To embrace the gifts he gave to share with all the words we talk
It is the Father who commands the land and sea
To live as one, respect the laws and rise so we are free
It is the Father we must pray and glorify
Be good to all he made and not destroy but realize
That the truth will never change with time
And we should follows paths to climb
And soon we all can be Divine…in love
It is the Father

It is the Son who showed us how to live
So that even the unfortunate will rise through His gifts
It is the Son that the Father spoke out loud
That we should follow in His steps deny the rich and proud
It is the Son who speaks with God's own blessed words
And we should cry out to the masses worshipping false gods
It is the Son and Jesus is His name
We must listen very carefully to each sentence and refrain
It is Jesus who is God's own Son
Who speaks the words with Blessed tongue and warns us of the doom and path
The need to listen and avoid…the wretched wrath
It is the Son

Believe In the Cross

The Holy Spirit who proceeded God and Son
Adored and glorified who lifted all to be as One
The Holy Spirit who spoke to prophets all
Of the need to tell the masses if they rise or if they fall
The Holy Spirit, the life and breath of God we know
Who empowers those who follow Jesus wanting just to grow
The Holy Spirit that brings conviction of one's faith
Bringing gifts of wisdom, understanding, knowledge, roads to take
The Holy Spirit, gifts of fear of the Lord
It is strength and fortitude and piety, the counsel of God
This is pure and simple, guides for all to relish all the words
The Holy Spirit

The Triune God which embraces all these three
It is Father, Son and Holy Spirit, one being eternally
The Triune God it's our faith we live each day
It's the teachings that have been passed down to those who want to pray
The Triune God that encompasses life throughout
It's the need to know we've done what's right, the urge to speak and shout
The Triune God, touching twelve who gave it all
Who followed in the footsteps knowing they would never fall
That our triumphs and prevails of life we'll walk through mud and sod
The success we'll feel at the end of life…
It's the Triune God.

This Soul is Yours

Richard Parnes

I was there on the edge of the world
Looking in at the sparks as they fly
Just to ask of the meaning of life
Is a page unanswered words from the sky
So I learned from masters with their prayers
To rise above my past will bare

Long before the nights
And long before the days were filled with
Sunshine in my life
And food to keep my nourished
I would feel the love inside
The peaceful cord that binds my soul with yours
You can understand
My drive to comprehend the meaning
Urge to know the land
The meditations and the feelings
Calmness of His voice and ever patient love that opens doors
This Soul is Yours

Just to hope of some divinity
As my lessons should be learned
For the answers they all lead to love
The rewards will be earned
And the story starts with each new birth
The goal is high, sustains its worth

Believe In the Cross

Long before the nights
And long before the days were filled with
Sunshine in my life
And food to keep my nourished
I would feel the love inside
The peaceful cord that binds my soul with yours
You can understand
My drive to comprehend the meaning
Urge to know the land
The meditations and the feelings
Calmness of His voice and ever patient love that opens doors
This Soul is Yours

Universal Consciousness of One

Richard Parnes

Many years ago there lived a gentle peaceful man
Tattered shoes he wore while walking in the desert sand
Didn't know if he could go on walking as he could
'til voices told him that he surely would

Be still my son the voice had said and listen to the words
Your inner strength will guide you to the land that you had heard
Your life will take new meaning as you soon will learn the way
To bring the fold you'll guide them and you'll say…

For all the learned ones come hear me as we sanctify our land
I've been told prosperity and peace is ours at hand
And we will be the envy for all to come and see
How Universal Consciousness of One will be

He took the words and vision and no longer felt the pain
The goals that he was given inner peace was his to gain
Soon many sects in all stood joined in one large crowd
And masses let their voices cry out loud

For all the learned ones come hear me as we sanctify our land
I've been told prosperity and peace is ours at hand
And we will be the envy for all to come and see
How Universal Consciousness of One will be

Believe In the Cross

We're here to be a part of one inspired plan
2000 years of peace from where we stand
Let's bring the word to see how true harmony should be
Our souls enlightened by our deeds, good karma sows the seeds

For all the learned ones come hear me as we sanctify our land
I've been told prosperity and peace is ours at hand
And we will be the envy for all to come and see
How Universal Consciousness of One will be

It Is Right

Richard Parnes

It is right to believe in the Lord Jesus Christ
It is right to follow in His words
It is right to pray to Him for all He has given
It is right to call out with spiritual swords

It is justice that God Almighty gave us His only Son
For He was chosen to lead us to the righteous path
It is justice to rise up and voice the truth
For those who do not believe will regret their troubled wrath

Bring forth the people to the holy gift of God
For we must reach out to all those in need
And those who only care for wealth and riches
Will regret the loss of the blessed seed

And time is finite when the end draws close
When we hear the sounds that we are at the end
For the reasons to follow in His commands
Will determine if we rise or shall descend

And when we stand before the gates of Heaven
Will our past show good or unforgiving?
Can we hope to enter blissful love and peace?
The joys of knowing eternal living

Believe In the Cross

It is right to believe in the Lord
God Almighty, Jesus Christ and the Holy Ghost
Our souls need the Holy Triune
We will succeed and will not boast

There's a path we all must truly follow
There's the good we must all reach for
There's belief in knowing only truth
We'll stand straight at our final door

And when we enter the eternal Heaven
And when we know our souls are complete
We'll continue on to glory
Praying all to conquer, wipe out defeat

It is right to believe in the Lord Jesus Christ
It is right to follow in His words
It is right to pray to Him for all He has given
It is right to call out with spiritual swords

If We All

Richard Parnes

If we all can agree to the path and the light
If we all can admit we were destined in true sight
To begin each morning, then take the lead while we talk
And the journey for our final day
If we strive to be good and to know of the Son
If we take hold of those who have only begun
We can show them commands and for those who believe
With the knowledge of truth while we pray

For the way of the heart is to follow His path
To eclipse all our sorrows throw away hateful wrath
Take the hands of others leading them in the light
Remove the blindfold opening eyes wide and bright
Also listen to God's words that came from His Son
Words of wisdom He spoke to all those at the mass
All those who believed now follow His way
Family, friends and neighbors who could never betray

Each morning rise to commit to the truth
Daily habits of work taking time always to pray
Precious moments in silence revering the Lord
Steadfast laws and commands that block hateful ways
For the glory of Heaven is the reward we shall reach
Mindful words that we utter within daily speech
Bring forth the way to the Lord and for all
Put Him in your daily life, this is your call.

Believe In the Cross

Tell a stranger the glory of the gifts that He brings
Raise your voices to God, Jesus Christ while you sing
If we all work together praising God and His Son
Wipe out negative passions that have hurt little ones
If we all take a stand to do only what's right
We can change all our enemies in the battles we fight
If we all want pure love with each day that's begun
We'll come together as family embracing His Son

Teach Me O Lord

Richard Parnes

Teach me O Lord the ways of the world
Open my heart and give me true Love
Give me the strength to shed the light you've provided to all
Wisdom and grace to give to the masses who stand straight and tall
Hold me so tight that I'll speak of the gifts you have given to me and to share with the world
Teach me O Lord the ways of the world

Let me provide to all those in need
Love for my neighbor is what you teach me
Care for the one who needs to believe and be shown the way
Give them the path to follow the road and never to stray
Guidance and strength and the messages told, give them the tools to plant all the seeds
Let me provide to all those in need

Sing a silent song
Say a prayer from your heart
Give it up to the Lord
Make a brand new start

Teach me O Lord the ways of the world
Let me provide to all those in need

Believe In the Cross

Many shall come and ask to be healed
All those believers as you are revealed
Take of the hands and tell them that others should come
Old lives are shattered, but new ones begun
Lighten the burden of souls who are poor, let the miracles happen as you did before
Many shall come and ask to be healed

Sing a silent song
Say a prayer from your heart
Give it up to the Lord
Make a brand new start

Teach me O Lord the ways of the world
Open my heart and give me true Love
Give me the strength to shed the light you've provided to all
Wisdom and grace to give to the masses who stand straight and tall
Hold me so tight that I'll speak of the gifts you have given to me and to share with the world
Teach me O Lord the ways of the world

Eternally

Richard Parnes

Stay with me.
I'm the one who loves you
I believe in you…Eternally
Stay with me
I'm the one who needs you
Pray and see…Eternally

You know all of my thoughts
You have heard all my dreams
There are moments each day that I want to scream to you
Take me away from corruption and crime
From the lies and deceit let me live for all time

Stay with me.
I'm the one who loves you
I believe in you…Eternally
Stay with me
I'm the one who needs you
Pray and see…Eternally

I long to travel with you to the ends of the Earth
To witness the awe of your miraculous birth
To stand firm and resolve
Be a part of the word
Make others believe that you're the Son of God

Believe In the Cross

Stay with me.
I'm the one who loves you
I believe in you…Eternally
Stay with me
I'm the one who needs you
Pray and see…Eternally (repeat)

So you created the world
Made a passion for life
It was up to man to live in love without strife
If we regard all the gifts from your only Son
We can all embrace the lives of each and everyone

Stay with me.
I'm the one who loves you
I believe in you…Eternally
Stay with me
I'm the one who needs you
Pray and see…Eternally (repeat)

Let the world come as one so we all can rejoice
The coming of the Lord, you'll know there is no other choice
Put down the evil and hate
We should choose only love
Rewards will be eternal when it's time to rise above

So, stay with me.
I'm the one who loves you
I believe in you…Eternally
Stay with me
I'm the one who needs you
Pray and see…Eternally (repeat)

Take Away

Richard Parnes

Take away the stars and the evening loses light
Take away the sun and the day's as dark as night
Take away the trees then the barren earth lays waste
Take away the seas and the land's as dry as paste

All the richness of His gifts will be removed of gold
All the blessings of the world the manifest be told
Somewhere in a distant land a sound is crying loud
People praying to the Lord the humbled ones are not proud

Let's be bold, confess our sins and speak so we are saved
Let's be bold to reach the poor to all who long and crave
Listen to our inner angels speaking words of God
Listen to the wisdom of the one and only Lord

All the teachings of the past are coming to be true
All the lies we've listened to no longer misconstrue
Take away our humbled hearts and evil spreads throughout
Take away our morals and the truth will become doubt

Let's become a people who will turn away from crime
Let us fight the ills of lies no longer waste the time
Turn ourselves into a world where love will surely dwell
Turn around the hatred as the Bible longs to tell

Believe In the Cross

Being one with God and Jesus gives us strength to show
Being one with Him lets the world to shine and glow
Manifest the good in all and shine throughout the world
Manifest the glory and all evil will unfurl

So don't take away the stars and the evening shines and glows
Don't take away the sun it's His gift that we all know
Don't take away the trees then the good green earth stands tall
Don't take away the seas the fish will multiply for all

All the richness of His gifts will crown the words throughout our speech
All the blessings of the world He gives that we will surly reach
Somewhere in a distant land our enemies we'll turn to love
People praying, joys of singing let us rise to stand above

So take away, don't take away our minds are rich within
So take away, don't take but say out hearts will stand with Him

In My Life

In my life I will always reach for you if I should fall
As I pray I will cast aside all doubts when I feel small
For Jesus loves me and I know He'll wipe away my fears
And He wraps His arms around my soul to wash away the tears

In my life I will face the world with those who stand with Him
I will walk with family greeting all and lights will never dim
For the days are numbered waiting for the coming to appear
As the lights ring bright the lamps are oiled wanting to be near

In my life there are moments when the masses will all pray
And our God will listen and His Son will stand to greet the day
When the day is over but tomorrow rings with blissful cheer
This is God's true love and we will walk and we'll rise to hear

In my life with the world still spinning He will gather all
They will walk or run and long to listen crowds are standing tall
And when it's time to meet our end our hearts spring love and care
'Cause its Jesus calling holding on He'll praise our final prayer.

I Pray to the Lord

Richard Parnes

I wake up early in the morning and I thank Him for my rest
He knows that the previous day wasn't one of my best
But I thank the Lord
For giving me another reason to be born
I know the lessens needed are to live, love and learn
Regard your fellow man with the kindness you would yearn
And thank the Lord
For credit due and the guidance to be shown
Plan for tomorrow, He's waiting there for you

I pray to the Lord, Bless in His name
He tells me to reap and to sow and to multiply
Then count all my gains
Take one day off, Bless in His word
I pray to the Lord

I want His hand to touch me every place that I go
I need good fortune following me as I grow
So I thank the Lord
For things are getting better with each year
I'll watch my every move recording it in my soul
The gifts I give to others are the lessons thus foretold
And I thank the Lord
His understanding ways to see and hear
Here come tomorrow, His slate and life of you

I pray to the Lord, Bless in His name
He tells me to reap and to sow and to multiply
Then count all my gains
Take one day off, Bless in His word
I pray to the Lord

My Abundance in Life

Richard Parnes

I've prayed to the Lord and have asked Him according
To the lessons I've learned very well
The tithes that I've given were not forced upon me
They increase the place that I dwell
He tells me to follow be humble not call on
The negative images spelled

These are the moments, my abundance of Life
This is the future my direction in life
He is my guidance to the path and the gold
I'll be His servant for the classes He'll hold

I have a propensity, urge for immensity
Things that are soon to unfold
Not meek, no they're giant and yet not defiant
Of causes that are labeled bold
To seek out the same, be on higher planes
To rise to occasions foretold

These are the moments, my abundance of Life
This is the future my direction in life
He is my guidance to the path and the gold
I'll be His servant for the classes He'll hold

The Lord is Close to Me

Richard Parnes

As I find myself left all alone
Should I worry what I'll think
I could feel so sorry for myself
I could lead myself feeling weak
But instead I search within myself
And I pray unto the Lord
Asking for conviction and for strength
Lead me on to fight with His word

So I'm blessed I know it
The Lord has been good to me
Lead me on in battle
I'll fight for victory
And the Lord is on my side
The battle fought with pride
Yes I'm blessed I know it
The Lord is close to me.

So with faith and love I know
I'll find that someone who would share
To continue on and no longer fight alone
Tell them beware
Since we've multiplied our forces
Let the battle hymns be heard
To the victor goes the spoils
Her the voices of the Lord

Believe In the Cross

So I'm blessed I know it
The Lord has been good to me
Lead me on in battle
I'll fight for victory
And the Lord is on my side
The battle fought with pride
Yes I'm blessed I know it
The Lord is close to me.

God's Pure Love

Richard Parnes

Lord don't you know
Of course you know everything
Take all of my pain away
The cause and effect that it brings
Lord can't you see
Of course you see everything
Open my eyes let me realize
That I can mend through harmony

And take of my hand
The shackles that band my heart and soul
And undo the grip
The coldness, the steel of the mold
Behold a new world
Where once stood the fear of its mass
And break into love
We'll form into lines, behold a new class
It's God's pure love

Let me be aware
Take anger away from me
Let me meditate
Then I will relate to you with no fear
Again be as one
Embrace all the gifts of His love
The peace radiates, our family is strong
He speaks to us from above

Believe In the Cross

And take of my hand
The shackles that band my heart and soul
And undo the grip
The coldness, the steel of the mold
Behold a new world
Where once stood the fear of its mass
And break into love
We'll form into lines, behold a new class
It's God's pure love

Déjà vu

Richard Parnes

Looking out my window I see so many things
What happened to the places that I knew?
The buildings look familiar, but I can't seem to place their names
Somebody tell me, I really don't have a clue
Who are these strangers? I recognize their names
Where did all my friends go? Lord tell me I'm not insane

Déjà vu. I thought I've been here before
Did I learn my lessons? My blueprint's my core
Did I hear my angels? Or am I just too crude?
I don't want to come back. I don't want Déjà vu

Spiritually! It seems to be alive
Even here, a different world from home
All appear to be learning. The Lord will survive
His teachings tell us don't do it alone
The world is rapidly changing. Let's prepare and meet the call
Give thanks for the learning. Let's bless the Lord for us all

Déjà vu. I thought I've been here before
Did I learn my lessons? My blueprint's my core
Did I hear my angels? Or am I just too crude?
I don't want to come back. I don't want Déjà vu

Walk a Mile to the Gates of Heaven

Richard Parnes

Walk a mile to the gates of Heaven
I want to see just what I've heard
Feel His strength and touch the beauty
That engulfs the Almighty Lord

Walk a mile to the gates of Heaven
I can't believe I'm gone right now
But when it's time to seek and do His bidding
I hope I'll give and show the masses how

There's understanding and patience from within
The cup's half full, have knowledge and have fun
Be humble, wise, lead not me to temptation
Forgive them for they know not what they've done

Walk a mile to the gates of Heaven
Let helping those be prior on my mind
And if I've done what I've been sent to deliver
Refrain from hurting all in humankind

Walk a mile to the gates of Heaven
I want to see just what I've heard
Feel His strength and touch the beauty
That engulfs the Almighty Lord

Believe In the Cross

The laws we've been given, the changes that we live
Makes no difference, the past returns to now
The facts that we've been here before, the hardships and the joys
God Almighty will never die I vow

Walk a mile to the gates of Heaven
I want to see just what I've heard
Feel His strength and touch the beauty
That engulfs the Almighty Lord

Maybe

Richard Parnes

Maybe I'll finally listen.
Open my senses inside
Maybe the angels will tell me
That I'm really making good stride
Maybe I'll see what tomorrow will bring
Or whatever happened to the very last spring
But then I will know that truly my heart means
To be all the best I can be

Maybe the sun will not warm me.
I wasn't the strongest last night
And maybe I'll walk in the shadows.
Bowing to my guilt and fright
But maybe I'll learn what I really should learn
Forgive all my faults and realize I'll earn
There's more to a life than just twenty-four hours
To be all the best I can be

I tried to forget that one word could damage
Or break one's pride
But lifting it up and knowing it's all right
To be by His side

So maybe I'll finally listen
And know that I'm doing my work
Maybe tomorrow will brighten
And roads will be paved to be walked
Maybe my dreams that were seeded with peace
Harvest the Oneness and evil will cease
Maybe just maybe, I'll know that humanity
Will be all the best it can be

Past Strife

Richard Parnes

What's deep in my soul? What am I hiding?
Why am I crying? Have I been told?
Will I accept? My past tells the story.
Was it for glory or should I regret?

All my thinking is wishful I should hold a fistful
Of words that I knew were so dear
Had I listened real closely I could have been only
Surpassing my previous fear
Then my present day's time would be spent in sublime
I'd be having the best of my life
Not repeating the faults and reliving the taunts
Of Past Strife

Some days there are moments. Sometimes it feels lonely
It would have been only a small favored prayer
And then there's that feeling from far away dreams
He's there so it seems and I know just where

All my thinking is wishful I should hold a fistful
Of words that I knew were so dear
Had I listened real closely I could have been only
Surpassing my previous fear
Then my present day's time would be spent in sublime
I'd be having the best of my life
Not repeating the faults and reliving the taunts
Of Past Strife

We Could Be Next

Richard Parnes

You should study the good book
You should quote from the verse in your text
You should pray to the Lord everyday for the good every way
You know darling, prepare yourself, we could be next

Look in the mirror what do you see? Are you pleased?
Have you any secrets? The Lord knows all in your mind
The meek shall rejoice for they're the ones who'll inherit the earth
The unbelievers they're the souls left behind

You should study the good book
You should quote from the verse in your text
You should pray to the Lord everyday for the good every way
You know darling, prepare yourself, we could be next

The Lord is all around he sees all that's been done
The brotherhood of man is God's creation
If we continue on the tracks of the harm that's begun
We could suffer more than starvation

You should study the good book
You should quote from the verse in your text
You should pray to the Lord everyday for the good every way
You know darling, prepare yourself, we could be next

You're the Rock I Need

Richard Parnes

Throughout all times you were on the minds of everyone
And each day that goes, the warmth inside grows in our hearts
Yet some will say pass, but those who amass the love of the soul
The giving of light, the spirit so bright will come and behold

To walk away now can never empower your destiny
Turn hatred away, you'll be led astray from your goal
So you will again, your path could have been the previous once before
Will you learn this time and figure your rhyme of what there is in store?

God you're the rock I need. You're the strength in all time
In peace and in war, throughout the folklore, the history of mankind
God you're the rock I need. The power that I shall find
When all's said and done, you're gift to be one, the learning's never blind
The soul is the seed
God you're the rock I need

The info at hand, you now understand the whys and hows
Learn patience and be secure and so free of all debt
Any maybe this time your last of a kind, your blueprint need not change
Your gift will arrive, you've earned to arise, a graduation met

God you're the rock I need. You're the strength in all time
In peace and in war, throughout the folklore, the history of mankind
God you're the rock I need. The power that I shall find
When all's said and done, you're gift to be one, the learning's never blind
The soul is the seed
God you're the rock I need

Come Alive

Richard Parnes

Love like a fire, burns in the wind
Yes there's desire there, the beauty from within
Yes there is spirit to grasp and to hold
The learning tree of life is there let it unfold

The knowledge and the guidance of the lessons of the Lord
The teachings not in classrooms, but inside where it's been stored
When the light turns on the sleeping child and you will feel reborn
Come Alive. Hear the Lord!
Come Alive, Live by His word.

High as a mountain and deep as the sea
The wonders He gives are there for you and me
But it can be taken and lost in a flash
When selfish pride awakens, what's left is only ash

We know that what we give in life returns as we receive
We learn that only hateful thoughts can fester and deceive
And when we question why and want love in pure form?
Come Alive. Hear the Lord!
Come Alive, Live by His word.

Believe In the Cross

When we should see that the truth can be a sword
Why is it hard not to see with open eyes?
Does it not feel good to walk in His steps?
Can't we know that with Him we'll live full lives?

The knowledge and the guidance of the lessons of the Lord
The teachings not in classrooms, but inside where it's been stored
When the light turns on the sleeping child and you will feel reborn
Come Alive. Hear the Lord!
Come Alive, Live by His word.

Because

Richard Parnes

Because that special moment when the world was standing cold and still
Life would take new meaning while the baby was kept from the chill
There would come a meaning that a future king was in their sight
Witnessed by those three who traveled following the light

Glory from the Father that His Son had entered into life
Angels prayed and spoke with calm to Joseph and his wife
The world became a better place knowing He was born
The future king would grow and learn passionate and strong

So there's a reason just sit and pray give all the thanks for Him
Because the light is beaming and will never cease or dim
Because the world is racked with strife and never seems to heal
Because destruction follow those whose lies would be revealed

And passion is the gift of those to bring about real change
Let's all embrace the truth He brings and cease to rearrange
If we should follow in His steps the glory we would feel
The joy sincere of happiness His gift would be our zeal

Because today is different and many fight their faith
The world in utter chaos where truth becomes disgrace
We're fighting for the freedom of those whose lives depend
The evil and lies persist until the bitter end

Believe In the Cross

Let's all embrace the truth in Him the Father, Holy Ghost
The Triune of the blessed Ones of those we cherish most
Become a world where only love shall manifest throughout
Because His words are everlasting filled with mighty clout

We all repeat our yesterdays we all live in the past
The lessons we were told to learn won't disappear they last
Because is just a simple word we sometimes throw away
Because is part of reason to get us through the day

So listen to the inner thoughts where Angels whisper to
And bless the Holy Trinity because…
Because…
They do love you

The Maker of the World

Richard Parnes

Last night I was in my room
I was praying to the Lord above
I was asking for the strength and hope
I was pleading, fill my heart with love
I was crying for all those in need
I was sighing please let them succeed
And He answered in a fatherly voice
And I listened as I had no choice
There were moments when all those who follow
With the chosen who would glorify His only son
And bow down to the One and only God.
The Maker of the World

So last night when I closed my eyes
I was thinking of the only Son
I was wishing He would touch my hand
I was dreaming life is finally done
I was drifting to the glory of light
I was seeing with the clearest of sight
And He gently took me in His grasp
With a firmness that was sure to last.
He told me it's not my time and this is only a dream it seems,
So understand this nod
When you bow down to the One and only God
The Maker of the World

Believe In the Cross

And this day when I woke from my sleep
I thought about the Blessed Son
I thought about Blessed Mary and Joseph
I thought about how life had begun
I thought about the twelve who were brought to His side
I thought about the twelve who would drop their pride
And the voices that were speaking to me
Informed that this was how it must be
They said be a part of forever at hand
And learn to listen and understand that this is your fortune
When you bow down to the One and only God
The Maker of the World

And this day when it's over and done
When you prepare again to go to sleep
When you lie still and say your prayers
When you Bless the Lord your soul to keep
When you genuflect, you give thanks to Him
When you bow your head and the light is dim
And the voices call speaking in your mind
That the world is better, understand and be kind
Knowing you're in line and you smile,
Still praying the rosary for awhile knowing this is you fortune
When you bow down to the One and only God
The Maker of the World

Let Me Follow

Richard Parnes

Let me follow in the path of God and Jesus Christ
I will not be deceived, the devil offers baneful ways
Let goodness follow me throughout all my time on Earth
My goal is Heaven, righteousness to carry me each day
Let the lives of Moses, Jacob and the chosen David shine on me
The wisdom given Solomon a gift I wish could be
I need for God to mold my soul so I could teach the child
And stress the goodness from His Son who walks strong and yet is mild

Let me follow widened roads to reach all those in need
I will not turn a scornful eye to those who seek to chide
Let me remember all He said to straighten out the ills I keep
I want to see the glory of the groom and beloved bride
Let the old and new be studied as the Bible plainly reads
The bad will simply wither while the good grow from strong seeds
Oh Lord I seek your words to carry me each and every day
I long to follow in your home to worship and to pray

Let me follow then let me swallow all arrogance and pride
I will not make a promise that I don't intend to keep
Let me carry hope and love and touch my neighbor's life
The good book that I carry is the riches that I reap
There are no secrets in my life, the Lord will know them all
If I don't try to make amends, He knows I'll surely fall
The days are passing quickly I will know when time is near
I hope He reaches for my hand and wipes away my fear

Believe In the Cross

So let me follow,
Please let me follow God and Jesus Christ
The miracle of Heaven...
I want eternal life

A Community of Love

Richard Parnes

Take all of my sins and wipe them away
 Oh Lord and Almighty God
Take all of my faults and let me repent to live a blessed day
Dear Lord and Almighty God
For I am a sinner and need to redeem
Learn to be tolerant helping those in need
As your teachings explain, require and glean the good in us all
The Lord will then see that we want and truly can be
A Community of Love

Let me be harmonious, sincere to lift toward the gate
Oh Lord and Almighty God
Respect fellow man and let go of hate
Dear Lord and Almighty God
You gave us the Son to show us the way
So our hearts can be changed and listen and pray
Remember the laws telling others to turn
That we long for sheer bliss, to grow and then yearn for
A Community of Love

So let us dance to the tunes of the spiritual songs
Oh Lord and Almighty God
Let us sing out and harmonize, join with the throngs
Dear Lord and Almighty God
The crowds long for oneness hoping for peace in the world
Discard false conclusions, the evil is hurled
The joy of pure passion with Him by our side
There's nothing to stop us our unity glides to
A Community of Love

Believe In the Cross

Let us take our disgrace and live in His peace
Oh Jesus and Almighty God
Taking each day to sit and to contemplate His grace
Oh Jesus and Almighty God
And we long just to move showing all of our might
Where others can grow, increase in the glory of His light
The beauty of Heaven, forever as we've heard
Open up the Holy book that lets us read the word towards
A Community of Love

This is the moment our redemption is near
Oh Jesus and Almighty God
Decisions and choices we'll choose love, hope and be clear
Dear Jesus and Almighty God
We will "Hear O' Israel" and steer towards His home
"Blessed be the Lord" for no other One will be shone
As we eat the sweet bread and then drink of the wine
It's contagious to pray, lift our hearts as He shines towards
A Community of Love

Let Me Be...
Your Song

Richard Parnes

I can awake and smile
The darkness is now gone
The sun has risen in the eastern sky
He knows my prayers and I belong
It's time to wash my face
The sleep that filled my eyes
To brush away the labored rest
Standing tall as I rise
Take me…Greet me… Let Me Be…Your Song

For the path has cleared for me to walk
And the roads are moving fast
When my destination comes in view
And my spirit longs for His firm grasp

So I can continue in the day
The sun fills me with warmth
Let me sit and thank Him for this moment
Still and reverent in my silence
Giving me more cheer
And filling in my time
To learn be free with precious memories
Regal and sublime
Take me…Greet me… Let Me Be…Your Song

So while I wash away all my past sins
To cleanse me move to the One
There's nothing more important than speak His word
Be kind give glory to His Son

Believe In the Cross

I close my eyes and smile and know
That I thank Him for this day
He knows my thoughts and movements
That are firm they never sway
The mother and the child
It's good to dream and think of Him
The vastness of the universe
His blessed star shall never dim
Take me…Greet me…Let Me Be…Your Song

Glory to God in the Highest

Richard Parnes

You see miracles done when a baby is born
When the mother has struggled to bring forth the child
You see life has begun with the first breath He takes
With His eyes opened wide and the gift from His smile
There's that road we must take as we walk to be near
For our lives long to see that each moment is blessed
With a hope that the words we have struggled to hear
Will be spoken and met so we never regress

Glory to God, Glory to God
Glory to God in the Highest (repeat)

With His arms opened wide He embraces us all
For the moment has come and we know we must stand
We have searched all our lives, we have sought out and prayed
And we've walked many miles throughout many lands
So to Him we reach out and we listen to hear
That God's glory erased all of our fear
He will wipe away doubt as we rise up above
We can conquer the hatred by bringing forth love

Glory to God ,Glory to God
Glory to God in the Highest (repeat 3x)

Believe In the Cross

So we all speak as one with commandments we say
It was brought down through lives to show us the way
There's the destiny calling the future unfolds
Just follow the bible as the message foretold

Glory to God, Glory to God
Glory to God in the highest (repeat 3x)

Son Our Lord

Richard Parnes

Yesterday's lonely
Tomorrow is only
Only for you, Son Our Lord
Wild geese that fly
Through a gray misty sky
I'm thinking of you, Son Our Lord
All of my dreams that I wanted it seems
Mean nothing since you came to me
Wanting to pray, thoughts of you night and day
I need you with me, Son Our Lord

Longing for you
Filled with feelings untrue
The strains of the day without prayer
Empty inside
And a loss of my pride
Standing hopeless if you are not there
Crying out loud feeling lost in a crowd
Would wipe away all of my hope
Being with you brings peace, dangers suddenly cease
Knowing time is a reason to cope

This is how it began
A miraculous plan
When the world was devised by our God
And all righteousness sings
With the wisdom He brings
To be near to Jesus our Lord

Believe In the Cross

So yesterday's passed
And the present won't last
For the future will shine with new clues
'Though the story repeats
With each day that retreats
And each mass that wipes away blues
Giving life to my soul, letting Him take control
Desires for Heaven and God
I need you dear friend, stay with me 'til the end
Your glory with me, Son our Lord

This is how it began
A miraculous plan
When the world was devised by our God
And all righteousness sings
With the wisdom He brings
To be near to Jesus our Lord

So yesterday's passed
And the present won't last
For the future will shine with new clues
'Though the story repeats
With each day that retreats
And each mass that wipes away blues
Giving life to my soul, letting Him take control
Desires for Heaven and God
I need you dear friend, stay with me 'til the end
Your glory with me, Son our Lord

A Thank You Prayer

Richard Parnes

Good morning God Almighty
Good morning Lord Jesus Christ
I thank you for another blessed day.
The sun is rising to warm the winter's chill
and my journey to your house is peaceful
 as I look forward to give you glory and pray.
May those who follow in my footsteps multiply to overflowing numbers
so that the voices ring out loud.
May your deeds and our prayers shake the evil souls who speak only of revenge
and are clothed in a darkened shroud.
Let the world be filled with kindness, love and compassion
to comfort those who are truly in need.
Let those who look past these wounded souls fall
because they wallow in their riches and in their greed.
Is it not your hope for mankind to rise
and glorify the Earth you gave?
This place on Earth as it is in Heaven
should remain sacred as all gifts we strive to save.
Remember all that you provide
and distribute to one and all.
Let us not trample on the weakened masses
Those who could not fight yet fall.
The world is the gift you give
the beauty we should harmonize and dance.
Let us always pray with the words you provide
and seek a second glance.
Dear Almighty God and Lord Jesus Christ
hear my thoughts and the words that I pray.
Thank you for the sun, the moon and stars
And thank you for today.

Author's Post Note:

With the ending of yet another page, I wish to thank those who have read my words. I thank God, Jesus Christ and my angels for providing the gifts to be able to express the feelings and hopeful that you, the reader, have enjoyed what was presented.

Go in Peace and Believe in the Cross.

www.ingramcontent.com/pod-product-compliance
Lightning Source LLC
LaVergne TN
LVHW091559060526
838200LV00036B/906